CONTENTS

How fast?

1 Speed is how far (the distance) something goes in a certain time. If a jet plane travels 3000 kilometres in three hours, its speed is 1000 kilometres per hour. We describe speed as distance covered – such as metres or kilometres – in one unit or 'piece' of time, such as one minute, one hour or one year.

2 Whether something is 'speedy' or fast depends on what, where and when. Cars on a motorway travel at 110 kilometres per hour. A garden snail crawls along at 18 centimetres per minute. The snail is 10,000 times slower than the car – but speedy compared to other kinds of snails.

3 We describe something as 'high speed' if it is very fast, but what we think of as high speed has changed over time. In 1972 the fastest sailing craft was *Crossbow*, a catamaran (yacht with two hulls), at 48.6 kilometres per hour. Just 30 years later the record was 103 kilometres per hour, due to the invention of kitesurfing, in which the sailor rides a modified surfboard while holding on to a special kind of kite.

▶ Some machines are not only built for speed, they are named after it. Speedboats such as these Vee-Class powerboats go faster than 160 kilometres per hour, their super-streamlined hulls slicing across the wave tops.

Steve Parker

Consultant: John Farndon

Miles
KeLLY

First published in 2012 by Miles Kelly Publishing Ltd
Harding's Barn, Bardfield End Green, Thaxted, Essex, CM6 3PX, UK

Copyright © Miles Kelly Publishing Ltd 2012

This edition printed 2014

10 9 8 7 6 5 4 3 2

Publishing Director Belinda Gallagher
Creative Director Jo Cowan
Editorial Director Rosie Neave
Volume Designers Dave and Angela Ball at www.da-designs.co.uk
Cover Designer Kayleigh Allen
Image Manager Liberty Newton
Indexer Gill Lee
Production Manager Elizabeth Collins
Reprographics Stephan Davis, Anthony Cambray, Jennifer Cozens, Thom Allaway

ISBN 978-1-84810-532-4

Printed in China

British Library Cataloguing-in-Publication Data
A catalogue record for this book is available from the British Library

ACKNOWLEDGEMENTS

The publishers would like to thank the following artists who have contributed to this book:

Julian Baker at J B Illustrations, Stuart Jackson-Carter, Mike Foster at Maltings Partnership

All other artwork from the Miles Kelly Artwork Bank

The publishers would like to thank the following sources for the use of their photographs:

t = top, b = bottom, l = left, r = right, c = centre, bg = background

Cover Front: Jon Feingersh/Blend Images/Corbis; Back: (t, bg) mmaxer, (cl) Sue Robinson, (cr) Andrey Yurlov

Corbis 4–5 Andy Newman/epa; 16–17 Thilo Brunner; 22(bl) PCN Photography; 26(bc) Bettmann; 36–37 Christopher Pasatieri/Reuters

Dreamstime 3(m) Joeygil

Fotolia.com 3 and 24–25(bg) Sharpshot

Getty 10(tr); 11(br); 13 Barcroft Media; 15(tr) AFP; 17(tc) Carsten Peter; 20–21 Dennis O'Clair; 23(b) AFP; 24(tr) AFP; 26(cl) Time & Life Pictures; 27(b) National Geographic; 28(tr) AFP; 30–31(b)

NASA 38(br) NASA Kennedy Space Center (NASA-KSC)

Nature Picture Library 12(cl) Robin Chittenden

Photoshot 14–15 UPPA

Rex 10–11 Sipa Press; 16(bl) Ashley Cooper/SpecialistStock/ SplashdownDirect; 21(tl) Claire Leimbach/Robert Harding; 22(br) KPA/Zumas; 28–29 Charles M. Ommanney; 29(t) Curventa; 34–35(b); 38–39 Everett Collection

Shutterstock.com 1 ssguy; 6(br) papkin; 6–7 Max Earey; 7(t) JetKat; 8–9(bg) Brian Weed; 8 nuttakit; 8–9(bg) somchaij; 9(br) Picsfive; 10(bc) Garsya; 10(bl) Edgaras Kurauskas; 11(tr) piyato; 15–16(c) Ahmad Faizal Yahya; 17(br) exclusive studio; 18–19 Kraska; 18(cl) vesna cvorovic; 19(br) Cathy Keifer; 23(t) alexkar08; 24(bl) Ralf Siemieniec; 27(tr) Graham Bloomfield; 30(tl) Germanskydiver; 30(br) MustafaNC, Péter Gudella; 30(bl) sabri deniz kizil; 31(tl) Pavel Kapish; 31(tr) dicogm; 34(tl) Andrei Marincas; 35(t) somchaij; 36(cl) helissente; 39(tr) bedecs

Science Photo Library 7(tr) NASA; 13(tr) David Parker; 25(br) NASA; 32–33(b) NASA; 33(cr) Peter Menzel

Topfoto.co.uk 28(bl) Topham/UPP

All other photographs are from:
Corel, digitalSTOCK, digitalvision, John Foxx, PhotoAlto, PhotoDisc, PhotoEssentials, PhotoPro, Stockbyte

Every effort has been made to acknowledge the source and copyright holder of each picture. Miles Kelly Publishing apologises for any unintentional errors or omissions.

Made with paper from a sustainable forest

www.mileskelly.net

info@mileskelly.net

Units for speed

4 Speed is the distance covered in a set time. A racing car might have a speed of 160 kilometres per hour for one lap of its course, but it might go at 300 kilometres per hour on straights and 50 kilometres per hour around bends. The 160 kilometres per hour is the average speed – total distance divided by total time.

$$SPEED = \frac{DISTANCE}{TIME}$$

6 The knot is used to measure how fast something goes on water. Its name comes from the fact that ships used to measure their speed by letting a rope out into the water. The rope had knots at regular intervals and a float at one end. The more knots that passed over the ship's side in 30 seconds, the faster the speed. One knot is equal to 1.83 kilometres per hour.

Knots

▶ Sailing speeds are still often measured in knots – as are wind speeds.

5 Throughout history, people have measured distance, time and speed in lots of different ways. Long ago, the time for a journey by sailing ship was measured to the nearest day, or even the nearest week! Today, modern jet planes mean the journeys are measured in kilometres per hour.

Miles
per hour
(mph)

▶ The speed indicator dial on fast cars may go up to 200 miles per hour.

Metres
per
minute

▶ For a snail or a slug, one metre is a very long distance.

7 Even today there are many different ways to describe speed around the world. In most of Europe, road speed is measured in kilometres per hour (km/h). In the UK and USA it is measured in miles per hour (mph).

Metres per second

▲ Comets travel through space at more than 66,600 metres per second, but seen from Earth, they appear to be hardly moving.

▶ Most passenger jet planes have a cruising speed of around 900–950 kilometres per hour.

Kilometres per hour (km/h)

8 To describe and imagine very fast or slow speeds, we have to change the measuring units we use. A rocket must reach more than 40,300 kilometres per hour to blast away from Earth into space. This is known as escape velocity. It may be easier to imagine as 11.2 kilometres per second, or even 11,200 metres per second.

9 Special units can help us when comparing speeds. A cheetah is much faster than a cockroach, but this is mainly because it is much bigger. However, if we compare each animal's speed to its size, things are rather different. A cockroach covers 50 of its own body lengths per second, but the cheetah covers just 12 of its own body lengths per second.

It's all relative

10 All speeds are relative. This is because nothing in the Universe is completely still. Even someone measuring speed is moving! So you can only measure something's speed 'relative' to something else – that is, by how fast it goes past.

11 A single object has many different speeds. A train goes at 100 kilometres per hour relative to its tracks and stations. For a person in a car travelling alongside the track at 60 kilometres per hour, the train's speed is 40 kilometres per hour. For a passenger on a train travelling towards the first train at 100 kilometres per hour, the combined speed is 200 kilometres per hour.

① To a person standing still at a station, the passing train's speed would be 100 kilometres per hour.

② For a driver in a car travelling alongside the train, its relative speed is 40 kilometres per hour.

③ For passengers in an oncoming second train, the combined speed is 200 kilometres per hour.

12 Usually we measure speed as the distance travelled here on Earth, along the surface or through the air – but this is also relative. The Earth's surface is moving as the planet spins once each day. If you could stay put in space, high above the Earth, someone standing still at the Equator (an imaginary line drawn around the mid-point of the Earth) would be moving at 462 metres each second.

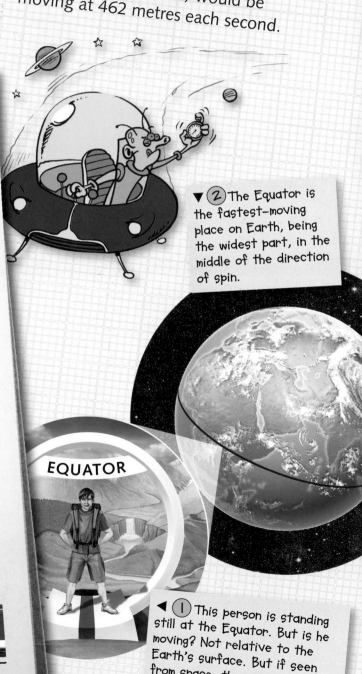

▼ ② The Equator is the fastest-moving place on Earth, being the widest part, in the middle of the direction of spin.

EQUATOR

◄ ① This person is standing still at the Equator. But is he moving? Not relative to the Earth's surface. But if seen from space, then yes – as fast as a jet fighter plane.

13 As well as constantly spinning, the Earth travels on its yearly orbit around the Sun. This makes working out speed even more complicated, since Earth's average orbital speed is about 30 kilometres each second.

▼ ③ Like the other planets, Earth zooms at huge speed around the Sun.

▲ ④ The Sun and millions of other stars are flying in space at gigantic speed, as the whole Galaxy swirls around.

14 Added to this is the speed of the whole Solar System (the Sun and all its planets). It is whirling around the centre of our massive group of stars, the Milky Way Galaxy. This speed is even faster – about 250 kilometres each second.

QUIZ

1. Is someone standing at the North Pole moving faster than someone standing at the South Pole?

2. What is Earth's average orbital speed?

3. Where should you stand to measure 'true' speed?

Answers:
1. No – they're equal (both spin around once every 24 hours)
2. 30 kilometres per second 3. There is nowhere you can stand.

15 Even if you went into deepest space, there is still nowhere that you can stand to measure 'true' speed. All the galaxies are flying away from each other, some at more than 300 kilometres per second. The whole Universe is moving faster and getting bigger.

Measuring speed

16 Long ago, there were no standard ways of measuring speed because there was no accurate way to measure time. People used devices such as sand clocks (in which sand poured through a small hole) to measure time, and methods such as counting their own steps to measure distance. The only way of comparing the speed of two or more things, such as horses, was a head-to-head race.

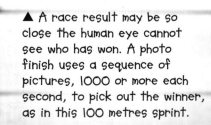
▼ The Olympics showcase the world's fastest humans in direct competition. Here Vomma Iso-Hollo wins 1932's 3000 metres steeplechase.

17 Gradually, measuring devices became more accurate. The first stopwatch was developed in the 1850s, and by the 1910s it was accurate to 1/100th of one second. During the 1970s, digital stopwatches increased this to 1/1000th of one second.

▼ Stopwatches used clockwork springs and measured to 1/100th of one second. Electronic timing devices use vibrating crystals to measure to 1/1000th of one second.

18 To measure distance, people once used lengths of wood. This gave rise to units of length such as the pole or rod, equivalent to 5.03 metres. Tape measures arrived in the 1700s, and by 1970 laser beams could measure distances more accurately.

▲ A race result may be so close the human eye cannot see who has won. A photo finish uses a sequence of pictures, 1000 or more each second, to pick out the winner, as in this 100 metres sprint.

19 For distance and speed over long distances, such as across seas, people relied on maps and charts. They measured the distance on the map and multiplied it by the scale of the map. But this was not very accurate – a very thin line on the map could be hundreds of metres wide in the real world.

20 From the 1990s the 'satnav' system GPS (which stands for Global Positioning System) meant speed over long distances could be measured much more precisely. GPS satellite clocks are accurate to 14 billionths of one second, and the best GPS receivers can pinpoint position to within 25 centimetres.

Each satellite transmits its identity and position

Some satellites are farther away, so signals arrive at the GPS unit at different times

GPS unit in vehicle is 'tuned in' to the signals from the satellites

▲ A 'satnav' receiver compares the times taken for signals to arrive from at least three GPS satellites.

21 Some sports have special ways to measure speed. The Hawk-Eye system uses several video cameras to record a ball's path from different angles. A computer compares the pictures and calculates the ball's speed and direction. A fast cricket bowl is 160 kilometres per hour, and a tennis serve can be 250 kilometres per hour – 70 metres in one second!

▼ In tennis, the Hawk-Eye tracking system shows the ball's speed, position and direction, and also if it landed on, in or outside the line.

OFFICIAL REVIEW

What is velocity?

22 Speed is distance covered with time — but it has no direction. To describe speed in a certain direction, we use the term 'velocity'. A swan might have a speed of 60 kilometres an hour when it migrates to its breeding area, but its velocity is 60 kilometres per hour due north.

23 Measuring velocity means measuring time and distance (as for speed), and also position. For long distances this can be done using GPS or 'satnav' equipment. In smaller areas it can be done with a map, perhaps using local landmarks, or with short-range radio signals such as radio beacons used by aircraft.

◄ This grey reef shark's radio tracker gives its position at different times, showing its overall velocity on longer journeys between reefs, and how, for example, ocean currents affect its movements.

24 Velocity gives much more information than speed. It shows changes in speed, direction and location, and how fast and how often they happen. This helps aircraft pilots to work out the fuel needed to climb to cruising height, go around storms, and circle or 'stack' waiting to land.

► As the plane passes through each criss-cross radio 'grid', the pilots work out its velocity to land safely.

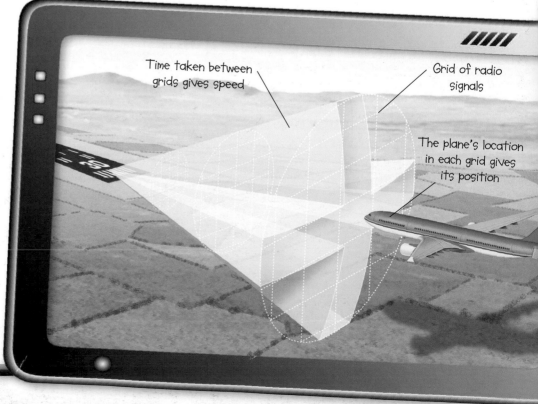

Time taken between grids gives speed

Grid of radio signals

The plane's location in each grid gives its position

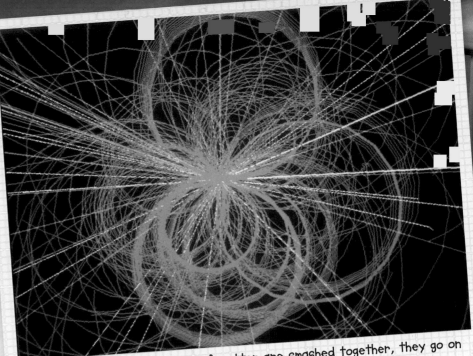

▲ When the smallest particles of matter are smashed together, they go on amazingly complicated curved pathways or tracks. These show their size, speed and structure.

25 On the huge scale of space travel, knowing about speed and direction, and so velocity, is vital. As a space probe sets off for a distant planet it must aim exactly in the right direction. Otherwise, after a journey of perhaps 10 years, it could be millions of kilometres off course. Space scientists continually check its path to keep it on target.

26 On the tiniest scale, velocity helps us to understand the world of atoms and their parts. These particles are smashed together with incredible force, such as in the world's largest machine, the LHC (Large Hadron Collider). The velocity of the resulting bits – their speed and direction – gives clues to their most basic make-up.

QUIZ

1. Rather than heading north, then the same distance east, what would be a quicker direction?

2. What is the name of the world's largest machine?

3. What is wrong with saying 'The car's velocity was 70 kilometres per hour'?

Answers:
1. Head north-east
2. Large Hadron Collider
3. You need to give the car's direction as well as its speed

◀ A US Air Force jet fighter watches space shuttle *Atlantis* on its final blast-off in 2011. The jet plane is capable of 2600 kilometres per hour. As the shuttle docks with the orbiting International Space Station, both the shuttle and the station will be travelling ten times faster. And both in the same direction – and so with the same velocity.

Speed and energy

27 Something that moves has not only speed, but also a form of energy – the ability to cause changes and make things happen. Energy due to movement or motion is called kinetic energy. You can see it at work everywhere – it is used to generate electricity from rushing river water and it is the reason that we have airbags and seatbelts in our cars.

29 Massively heavy things are more difficult to speed up. They have high inertia, which means they need lots of energy to give them motion. The heavy flywheel in an engine needs great force to get it going, but once it's spinning, it helps the engine run smoothly.

▶ One very strong human – Mikhail Sidorychev – can gradually overcome the inertia of a huge plane, giving it kinetic energy to get it moving.

28 Kinetic energy depends on two main features – an object's speed, and its mass (amount of matter). The faster something goes, the more kinetic energy it has, and the more mass it has, the more kinetic energy it has. So a very fast motorbike could have the same kinetic energy as a very slow truck.

HOW FAR?

You will need:

tennis ball   stiff card about 60 cm long
pen   measuring tape

1. Draw a scale on the card, marking every 2 cm. Prop up one end of the card at an angle of about 30° to make a ramp.
2. Release the ball from each mark in turn. Measure how far it rolls each time. The ball gains more speed from each higher mark, and so has more energy to roll farther.

▼ On a 'Wall of Death', fast-circling riders produce enough outward force to overcome gravity and rise at right angles up the wall.

30 Once an object is moving with speed, it has lots of kinetic energy, or high momentum. Then it resists losing speed – being slowed down. A huge, speedy ship such as an oil tanker has so much momentum that it may take 50 kilometres to slow down.

▼ Racing bikers have to learn how to slow down and lean into corners.

31 As an object goes around a bend or curve, it has different forces acting on it, and this affects its speed. A motorcycle can go fast in a straight line, but around a bend it must slow down as the rider leans to one side so that its tyres don't lose grip and skid.

32 Spinning at speed causes another set of forces. One is felt as a pull away from the centre of the spin. This is known as centrifugal force, and is used in machines called centrifuges. A medical centrifuge spins tubes of blood so fast, the heaviest parts sink to the bottom of the tube. This helps to separate blood into its different parts.

Natural speeds

33 The natural world has a huge range of speeds, from incredibly slow to ultra-fast. Some of the slowest movers are the world's landmasses or continents. They drift around the planet's surface by a few centimetres each year.

34 Glaciers are thick 'rivers' of snow and ice. They slide downhill, mostly by a few metres each year. In Greenland, the Jakobshavn Glacier sped along at more than 12 kilometres per year, probably due to global warming.

35 Rivers have many different speeds, from 10-plus metres per second down steep rapids to less than one metre per minute in other places. The giant Amazon River's average flow speed is about 2 kilometres per hour. One of the fastest ocean currents is the Agulhas Current in the Indian Ocean, at 10 kilometres per hour.

▼ Where a river flows through a narrow gorge, it speeds up as rapids. The same amount of water passes every second as in places where the river is less restricted.

10 m/second

12 km/year

▼ A scientist using an instrument called a theodolite. This records the exact position of marker poles at certain times to determine a glacier's speed.

36 In 1980, the eruption of Mount St Helens, in the north-west USA, caused an avalanche and rockfall that travelled at more than 400 kilometres per hour. This was one of the fastest ever measured. Even a small avalanche can reach 120 kilometres per hour, which is much too fast to outrun.

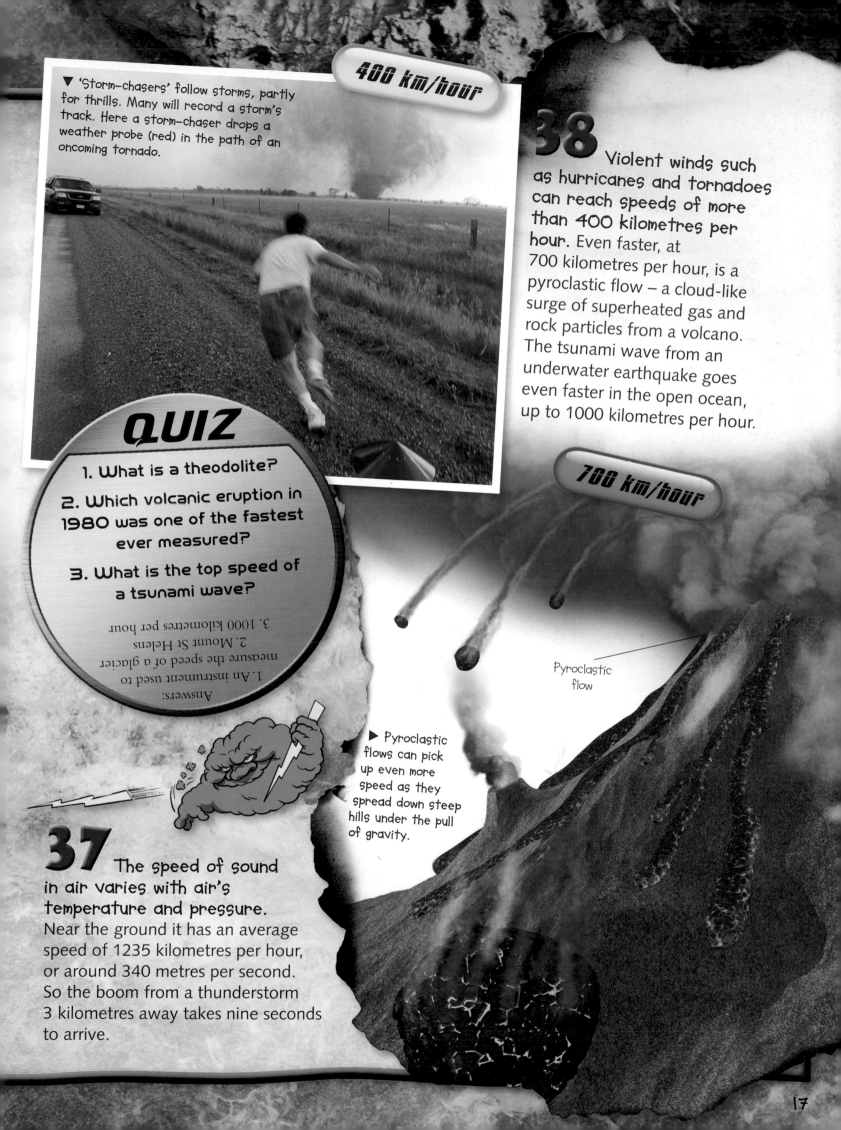

▼ 'Storm-chasers' follow storms, partly for thrills. Many will record a storm's track. Here a storm-chaser drops a weather probe (red) in the path of an oncoming tornado.

400 km/hour

38 Violent winds such as hurricanes and tornadoes can reach speeds of more than 400 kilometres per hour. Even faster, at 700 kilometres per hour, is a pyroclastic flow – a cloud-like surge of superheated gas and rock particles from a volcano. The tsunami wave from an underwater earthquake goes even faster in the open ocean, up to 1000 kilometres per hour.

700 km/hour

Pyroclastic flow

▶ Pyroclastic flows can pick up even more speed as they spread down steep hills under the pull of gravity.

37 The speed of sound in air varies with air's temperature and pressure. Near the ground it has an average speed of 1235 kilometres per hour, or around 340 metres per second. So the boom from a thunderstorm 3 kilometres away takes nine seconds to arrive.

Life in the fast lane

39 An animal's speed depends on the environment in which it is moving. The sailfish cuts through water at 110 kilometres per hour. The cheetah sprints on land at about the same speed. The peregrine falcon is the fastest of all animals – its stoop or 'power dive' through the air can reach speeds of over 300 kilometres per hour.

300 km/hour

Part-folded wings lower air resistance

40 Cheetahs are famously fleet-footed, but there are lots of other speedy creatures. The fastest reptile is the spiny-tailed iguana lizard, which runs at 35 kilometres per hour. The speediest shark – the short-fin mako – swims at more than 60 kilometres per hour, while the fastest mammal swimmer is the killer whale or orca at 55-plus kilometres per hour.

Small head for streamlining

Flexible backbone

110 km/hour

Tail works as an air rudder to change direction

Powerful muscles in shoulders and hips

▲ The cheetah's long, slim, flexible body and long legs allow it to cover 8 metres in each bound.

41 Animal adaptations for speed on land include long legs for lengthy strides, and powerful muscles in the shoulders and hips. In water, fast fish such as marlin have stiff, crescent-shaped tails that they thrash from side to side so fast, they look like they are quivering.

Stiff, narrow, curved tail

42 One of the fastest muscle actions in the animal world is the mantis shrimp's club-like pincer or claw. It 'locks' in a bent position using a trigger-like part, builds up muscle force, and then 'unlocks' to throw a punch that lasts less than 1/200th of a second, moves at 22 metres per second, and strikes with the force of a rifle bullet.

◀ The peregrine does not simply fall downwards in its stoop. It flaps its wings for even greater speed.

Wing feathers fanned for greater push

43 Inside living things, one of the fastest actions is the movement of nerve signals. They can travel at more than 100 metres per second, going from human toe to brain in less than 1/50th of one second.

44 Plants can be speedy too. The venus flytrap flicks its leaf shut around an insect victim in less than half a second. Plants such as giant kelp seaweed and some types of bamboo grow at great speed – up to one metre each day.

110 km/hour

Top (dorsal) fin folds down at speed

Pointed snout for less water resistance

▲ Blocks of powerful muscles along the sides of the sailfish's body swish its tail from side to side, and make up more than three-quarters of the fish's weight.

▶ If this fly touches the trigger hairs near the hinge of the venus flytrap's leaf, the trap at once snaps shut.

Breeding the best

45 People have held races to find the speediest animals and people for more than 5000 years. Early races involved horses, camels, dogs and humans. Running and chariot racing were among the most popular events at ancient Greece's Olympic Games, 2500 years ago.

46 Some of the biggest prizes are given for the fastest racehorses. Perhaps the quickest was Secretariat, an American thoroughbred that raced in the 1970s. He set records that still stand today, winning the 1973 Kentucky Derby at 16.8 metres per second (60 kilometres per hour).

47 People can select the fastest animals of each kind, and breed them together to produce even speedier ones. This process is called selective breeding. It has produced the fastest type of dog, the greyhound. It races at almost 20 metres per second (72 kilometres per hour) – nearly twice as fast as a human sprinter.

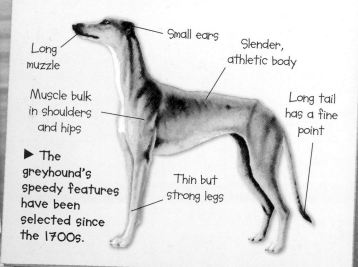

Long muzzle

Small ears

Slender, athletic body

Muscle bulk in shoulders and hips

Long tail has a fine point

Thin but strong legs

▶ The greyhound's speedy features have been selected since the 1700s.

▼ Fast-action photos show how a racehorse's leg-moving muscles are concentrated in the shoulder and buttock areas. Most of the leg is slim and easy to swing fast.

▲ The fastest camels are almost as rapid as racehorses, reaching speeds of over 55 kilometres per hour.

50 Training a champion animal speedster is a complicated business. Trainers pay great attention to diet and exercise, working out a series of activities that build gradually to the day of the big race. Some racehorses only run well if they have their 'best friend' stable companion with them on the day – which might be a donkey!

48 Many animals are raced for speed and stamina (endurance). Strange races include camels, ferrets, maggots, elephants, sled–pulling husky dogs, hamsters in wheeled cars, and pigs with pretend stuffed–toy 'jockeys'. Elephants weigh over 5 tonnes yet they can reach speeds of 6.6 metres per second (24 kilometres per hour).

49 Breeders look for several features in racing animals. These include a slim but muscular build, strong bones (especially in the legs), no spare fat, a strong heartbeat, and clear breathing to take in the oxygen in air needed by hard-working muscles.

>>>>>>>>

WORM OLYMPICS

You will need:
earthworms   A4 paper
sticky tape

1. Roll and tape sheets of A4 paper into tubes about one centimetre wide.
2. Tape the paper rolls side by side.
3. Carefully gather garden earthworms and put each one into a tube at the 'Start' end.
4. The worm that is first to emerge completely at the 'Finish' end is the winner!

Note: After your race, put the worms back in the soil where you found them and wash your hands.

>>>>>>>>

Out in front

51 **Human speeds improve year by year.** In 1912 the record time for the 100 metres sprint was 10.6 seconds. Today it is more than one second less. This is partly because people have generally become healthier, with better food and fewer illnesses, especially in childhood. We also understand more about exercise and how the body works.

53 **Human speeds have also increased for money reasons.** Modern sport is big business that attracts the best brains to train athletes. Coaches devise incredibly detailed training programmes covering everything from building muscle and improving breathing, to planning their athlete's mental approach to each race.

▶ From 2008, Jamaica's Usain Bolt shattered sprint records and became World and Olympic champion at 100 and 200 metres, at speeds of up to 37.5 kilometres per hour.

Strong bone structure

Efficient lungs and heart

Slim arms

Narrow hips and slim legs

Minimal body fat

Powerful pump-action arms

Tall stature

Muscle bulk in hips and legs

Long legs for extended stride

52 **Some people have innate (inbuilt) features, which help them to run fast.** Being tall and muscular with long legs is ideal for short-distance sprinting. A smaller, slimmer, lighter build is more suited to long distances.

◀ Britain's Paula Radcliffe has the narrow, lightweight shape of a long-distance runner. She took the world marathon record in 2003 at an average speed of 18.7 kilometres an hour.

54

Every so often, a great landmark or 'milestone' is reached in human speed. In 1954 English runner Roger Bannister was the first person to run a mile in less than four minutes – which many people said was impossible. In 1968 Jim Hines of the USA broke the '10-second barrier' and ran the 100 metres sprint in 9.9 seconds.

▶ When Bannister broke the four-minute mile, people doubted the time could reduce much more. Today's runners are 15 seconds faster.

▼ In 100 years, the record time for the 100 metres freestyle swim – here with modern French champion Alain Bernard – has reduced from 66 to 46 seconds.

55

There are lots of different human speed records. These range from the 60-metre 'flying start' and sprints at 100, 200 and 400 metres, to middle-distance 800 and 1500 metres, and long-distance 5000 and the marathon (42,195 metres). If sprint swimmers in a 50 metres front crawl race could maintain their speed over 1500 metres, they would cut the record time for that race (currently 14 minutes and 30 seconds) by four minutes!

Designed for speed

56 The quest for speed has led people to design, build and operate all kinds of speed machines. From soap-box carts and penny-farthing bicycles to racing cars, powerboats, jet trucks, bullet trains and rocket planes – as with human speed, machine speed keeps improving through the years.

Slippery body suit fabric

Contoured helmet

Arms and hands together

Spokeless disc wheels

▲ Track cyclists use every design trick to reduce air resistance or drag.

57 One important feature of a speed machine is its overall size. Bigger is usually faster, but only up to a certain point. A larger machine can have a bigger, more powerful engine, but the weight of the machine itself, with its frame and working parts, increases greatly and speed becomes slower again.

Bonnet 'flows' into windscreen

Mirrors close to body

▶ Air is pushed over a car smoothly, rather than being allowed to go underneath and lift it at high speed.

Low sloping front

Rounded front wheel arches

◀ A hydrofoil lifts up at speed to reduce drag on its hull.

58 'Drag' is the enemy of speed. Drag is the resistance or pushing-back force from air or water, as an object shoves between its tiny particles or molecules. A speed machine is shaped to be streamlined or 'slippery' with a pointed front, smooth surfaces and curves, a tapering rear end, and no sticking-out parts.

59

Before building a speed machine, design models can be tested in wind tunnels or water tanks. This shows how the air or water flows past the vehicle. It reveals any swirls, eddies (circular movements) or vortexes (unsteady movements), which may increase drag and have a slowing effect.

Gradual rear slope

Rear wing presses down back wheels for better grip

Minimal airflow under car

60

Speed machines cannot be totally smooth and streamlined, because they need to move in a steady, stable, safe way. So they may have ridges, fins or wings that act like wings in reverse, pushing the car's wheels down onto the ground for extra traction (grip).

61

Computers also help to design speed machines. A virtual design, existing only in the computer, can be put into a virtual wind tunnel or water tank, also in the computer, to see how it performs. By pressing a few keys the designers can redesign a part to try and improve performance.

▶ Computer modelling shows how swirling air currents are 'thrown off' the rear parts of a fast plane, slowing it down.

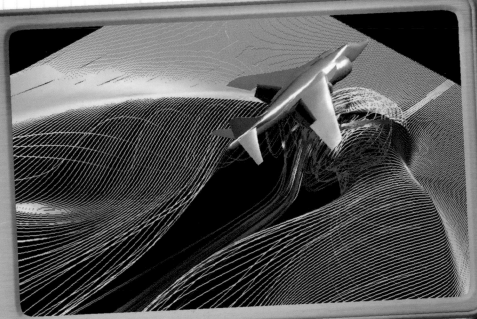

Making a breakthrough

62 Through history, different types of speed machines have got faster by small amounts. A big leap in performance is usually the result of a new invention or development, such as a new engine, better materials that save weight, or a new control method, such as a computer.

▼ *Railton Mobil Special*, driven by John Cobb, was the last piston-engined vehicle to hold the world land speed record.

63 In the early 1950s a new kind of propeller-driven speedboat made a huge splash. *Slo-Mo-Shun IV* used a method called prop-riding, where the boat's hull rose at speed to lift the top parts of the propellers above the surface. This reduced their pushing force but reduced drag even more. It improved the water speed record by 60 kilometres per hour in two years, to 287 kilometres per hour.

▼ *Spirit of America* became the first jet car to take the land speed record, powered by an old GE J47 engine from a Sabre jet fighter plane.

64 In the late 1940s the world land speed record was held by John Cobb in *Railton Mobil Special*, at 634 kilometres per hour. This vehicle had piston engines that turned the wheels, like an ordinary car. By 1965 the record had shot up to almost 1000 kilometres per hour with Craig Breedlove in *Spirit of America*, due to the arrival of the jet engine.

FASTEST OR FARTHEST?
You will need:
computer   printer   A4 paper
1. Go to www.factsforprojects.com and click on the paper aeroplanes link.
2. Make two planes – the Condor is like Concorde and the Bullet is like the X-15.
3. Test them outdoors on a calm day. The dart goes fastest, but the glider may stay up longer and fly a greater distance. It's not always fastest that goes farthest.

65 In 1938 the steam locomotive *Mallard* set the speed record for railed vehicles, at 202.6 kilometres per hour. Then along came electric trains, which soon pushed the record higher, and by 2007 it was over 570 kilometres per hour. Maglev trains, which 'float' above rails, go even faster.

Front view of train

Track levitation magnet

Close-up

Section through rail

Train levitation magnet

Train guide magnet

▲ Maglev trains use magnetic levitation – magnetic forces that suspend the train over the track, removing the problem of wheels and friction.

▲ Concorde was the fastest-ever passenger aircraft. But fuel costs, noise and old age led to it being retired in 2003.

67 The invention of the jet engine had a huge effect on aircraft speed records. The fastest propeller plane was probably the Russian Tu-114 passenger aircraft of the 1960s, at 870 kilometres per hour. By 1969 jet-powered Concorde had more than doubled this to 2172 kilometres per hour. Today jet fighters reach 3300 kilometres per hour.

66 The fastest of all powered machines have rocket engines. In 1967 the USA's X-15 rocket plane reached 7273 kilometres per hour, which is still a record for any manned vehicle or craft – apart from in space. Returning from the Moon in 1969, Apollo astronauts reached 40,000 kilometres per hour.

▲ The X-15 was launched in mid air from a giant bomber aircraft. Two X-15 flights zoomed for a few seconds to the edge of space, over 100 kilometres high.

Modern speed machines

68 Apart from kitesurfers and windsurfers, the fastest sailing craft is *Hydroptère*. It has one main hull and two smaller outer hulls, and is a hydrofoil, rising up at speed on wing-like struts. The craft took the record in 2009 with a speed of 97.9 kilometres per hour.

69 In 1997 the UK's jet car *Thrust SSC* roared across Black Rock Desert, USA to set the land speed record of 1228 kilometres per hour. It was driven by fighter pilot Andy Green, with former record-holder Richard Noble as team boss. 'SSC' stands for Super-Sonic Car, because the vehicle also broke the sound barrier as it set the record.

▲ *Hydroptère* made several failed attempts on the water speed record — during one of which it almost sank — before its 2009 success.

▲ *Thrust SSC* caused a sonic boom as it scorched across Nevada's Black Rock Desert, on its record-breaking two-way run.

70 In 1978 the world water speed record of 511.1 kilometres per hour was set by Ken Warby in his home-made, jet-powered craft, *Spirit of Australia*. It was on Bowering Dam, Australia, with perfect conditions of wind and water surface. This record is one of the most dangerous, and two attempts to break it have killed the pilots. Warby's record still stands.

▲ Warby built *Spirit of Australia* in his garage, using a second-hand jet engine given by air force friends.

71 To design, build, test and run a new record–breaking speed machine costs huge amounts of money. This is one reason why main speed record attempts are rare. Teams hoping to take the land speed record include the UK's *Bloodhound*, the North American Eagle Project and Australia's *Invader 5R*.

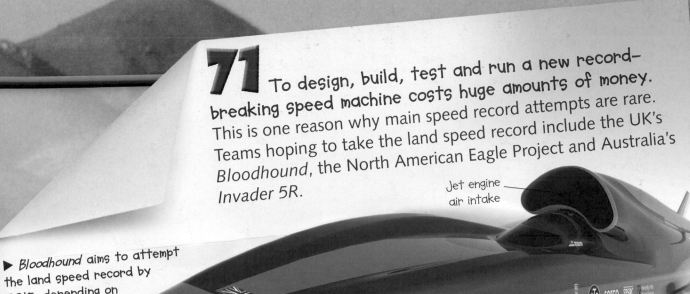

Jet engine air intake

Stabilizer wing

Nose wheel

▶ *Bloodhound* aims to attempt the land speed record by 2015, depending on how much money is raised.

Pointed nose

QUIZ

1. Which is faster, a jet-powered car or one with an ordinary engine?

2. Which country holds the land speed record with Thrust SSC?

3. Where were the first 'bullet trains' – Peru, Japan or Barbados?

Answers:
1. A jet-powered car
2. UK 3. Japan

72 Apart from trains specially altered to break records, there are also records for the fastest regular or scheduled railway service. In 2011 a new type of train – called a 'bullet train' because of its shape and speed – linked the Chinese cities of Beijing and Shanghai. It carries 500 people and can reach 480 kilometres per hour.

73 To get away from the vast cost of breaking the all-out best speed, there is increasing interest in human-powered craft and vehicles. There are records in the air, on land and water, and even underwater. The human-powered submarine *Omer 5* set the underwater record in 2007, at 14.9 kilometres per hour.

Reaching the limit

74 Speeds cannot keep increasing forever. To break the land speed record, *Thrust SSC* needed an incredibly flat surface and a straight course of almost 20 kilometres. Faster cars will probably need longer courses, until the Earth's landscape is the limit.

◀ Skydivers move their arms, legs and body position to speed up or slow down. The belly-to-earth position gives a fall speed of 190 kilometres per hour.

75 As an object goes faster, the opposing drag or resistance rises too, at an ever-increasing rate. Eventually, resistance equals forward force, and the speed limit (terminal velocity) is reached. As parachutists free-fall to Earth, they are pulled by gravity but slowed by air resistance. When these forces balance the parachutist has terminal velocity, which is about 200 kilometres per hour.

76 Speeds are limited for safety reasons. On roads in built-up areas, the UK speed limit is usually 30 miles per hour. Accident information shows that at this speed, about one person in ten hit by a car dies. At just 10 miles per hour more, nine in ten die.

▼ Stopping distance increases in proportion. At 60 miles per hour, it is over three times more than 30 miles per hour, not twice.

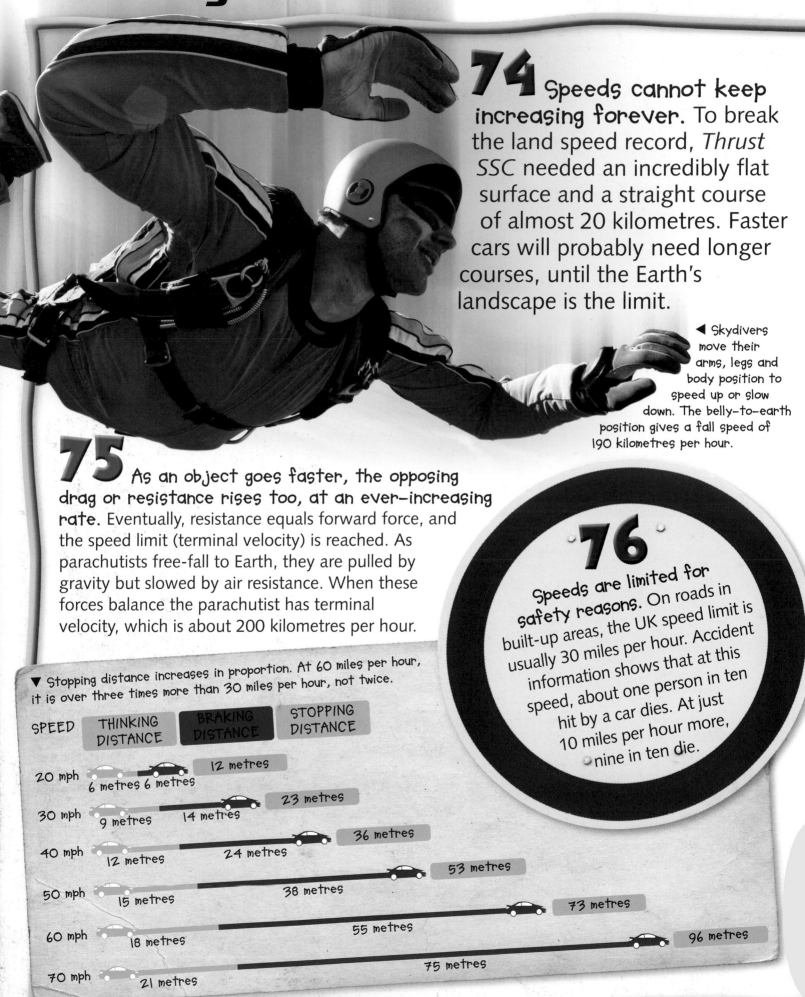

SPEED	THINKING DISTANCE	BRAKING DISTANCE	STOPPING DISTANCE
20 mph	6 metres	6 metres	12 metres
30 mph	9 metres	14 metres	23 metres
40 mph	12 metres	24 metres	36 metres
50 mph	15 metres	38 metres	53 metres
60 mph	18 metres	55 metres	73 metres
70 mph	21 metres	75 metres	96 metres

◄ A car's rev counter warns of danger above 7000 rpm. This is when the engine is turning more than 115 times each second.

77 Engines, motors and other machines have speed limits for their moving parts. Otherwise damage is likely as parts spin or move so fast that they crack and shatter. Many cars have a dial showing engine rpm – revolutions (turns) per minute. The high end of the dial is coloured to warn against making the engine turn so fast.

▼ Formula 1 car engines turn at up to 18,000 rpm. At this speed, if one tiny engine part fails, the whole engine may shatter and catch fire.

78 Computers may seem the fastest machines, but even they have their limits. They work by moving particles called electrons, which are pieces of atoms, in the form of tiny pulses of electricity. But electrons need energy to push them along, and they have a maximum travel speed. The upper limit may be reached in 15–20 years.

ROLLER SLIDE RACES

You will need:
children's play slide   string
pair of roller skates
objects of different weights

1. Choose two items of different weights and tie one to each skate.
2. Let both skates go from the top of the slide at the same time. Note which one reaches the bottom first.
3. Repeat for several objects. Does the heaviest one always win?

Speeding up, slowing down

79 Hardly anything goes at a steady speed – not even planets travelling around the Sun. The Earth's speed varies by more than 3600 kilometres per hour between the fastest and slowest part of its orbit. Movement always involves speeding up, called acceleration, and slowing down, or deceleration.

▼ Top Fuel dragsters are the fastest-accelerating cars. From standstill, they cover a one-quarter-mile track in five seconds, finishing at a top speed of over 500 kilometres per hour.

80 The rate of change for speed is measured by how the distance covered in a certain time changes with time. A car starts from standstill, goes one metre per second after one second, two metres per second after two seconds, and so on. Its rate of acceleration, or speeding up, is one metre per second per second. This is usually written as m/s^2.

▲ This car speeds up from standstill to 60 miles per hour in ten seconds. So its average rate of acceleration is 6 miles per second per second, or 6 miles/sec².

81 Speeding up and slowing down are caused by a change in force, such as an engine turning faster or wind blowing harder. A familiar example is when something falls to Earth's surface under the force of gravity. In theory, this causes an acceleration of 9.81 m/s^2, often known as the 'g force'. In reality, air resistance reduces this acceleration.

▶ Lieutenant Colonel John Paul Stapp experiences extreme g forces during a rocket-propelled acceleration and deceleration exercise in which he reached 1017 kilometres per hour in five seconds.

At standstill

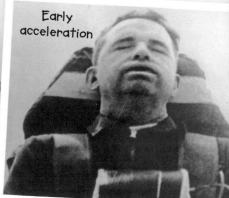

Early acceleration

82 Bigger planets than Earth have much stronger forces of gravity, so their g forces are higher. On the largest planet, Jupiter, falling objects would accelerate at 25 m/s². On the Moon, which is much smaller, this would be 1.6 m/s².

83 Accelerometers measure how fast things speed up or slow down. Most contain small crystal-like parts that change shape slightly as their rate of movement alters, producing tiny amounts of electricity. Two of these devices at right angles can track the direction of a movement, as well as acceleration.

▲ If a micro-accelerometer (seen on the hand at the front of the image) detects a car's sudden slowdown, the safety airbag inflates in one tenth of one second.

84 Accelerometers are used in hundreds of everyday objects, from airbags in cars to the hand-held controllers for computer games and mobile phones. They are also used to detect motion in volcanoes and cliffs that might warn of eruptions, earthquakes and rockfalls.

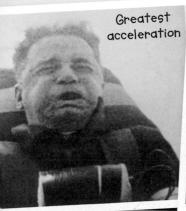
Greatest acceleration

Top speed

Beginning to decelerate

Greatest deceleration

33

Stop!

85
What speeds up, eventually slows down. Less speed, or deceleration, is a vital part of working machines, motors and engines. To save time and stay safe, many of them have specially designed ways of slowing down.

86
Some kinds of brakes use drag or resistance. Fast planes have air brakes – flaps on the wings or body that fold out into the passing air to increase drag. Very fast planes release a parachute at the rear when they need to slow down fast, for example when landing on an aircraft carrier.

▶ On a short runway, the F–117 Nighthawk stealth fighter uses a parachute as an airbrake, to help it slow down when landing. This saves wear on the wheels, tyres and brakes.

87
Brakes are a common way to slow down. Most use rubbing or friction, which converts kinetic energy (the energy of movement) into heat energy. Many cars have disc brakes, in which stationary pads on the car rub against a disc attached to the road wheel. In many types of electric saw the spinning blade is 'grabbed' by a friction device to slow it down fast when the motor is switched off.

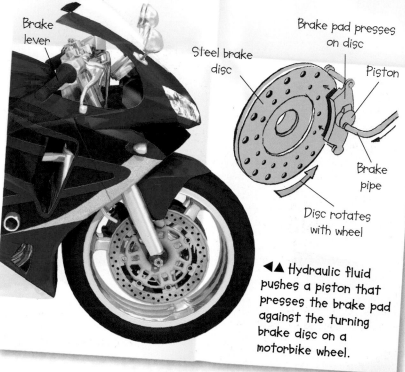

Brake lever

Steel brake disc

Brake pad presses on disc

Piston

Brake pipe

Disc rotates with wheel

◀▲ Hydraulic fluid pushes a piston that presses the brake pad against the turning brake disc on a motorbike wheel.

88 If the driver of a speeding car brakes too hard, the wheels may lock and skid, so the vehicle goes out of control. A car's ABS (anti-lock braking system) senses this and makes the brakes 'pulse' on and off many times each second, under computer control. This prevents wheel lock and slows the car more safely.

Full-face helmet

Mesh across the window prevents the driver's arm from going through the window in the event of a crash

Sides of seat curve around the driver's ribcage while straps keep him or her securely in position

Flameproof suit

Roll cage made from steel tubing

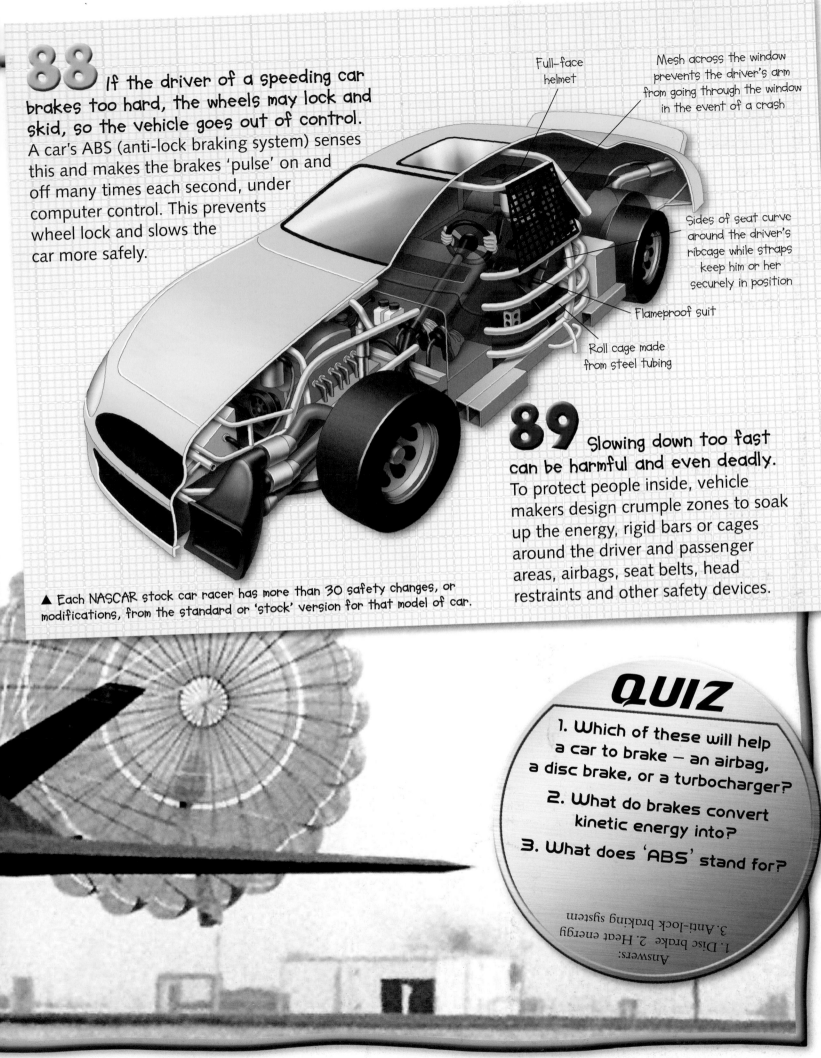

▲ Each NASCAR stock car racer has more than 30 safety changes, or modifications, from the standard or 'stock' version for that model of car.

89 Slowing down too fast can be harmful and even deadly. To protect people inside, vehicle makers design crumple zones to soak up the energy, rigid bars or cages around the driver and passenger areas, airbags, seat belts, head restraints and other safety devices.

QUIZ

1. Which of these will help a car to brake — an airbag, a disc brake, or a turbocharger?

2. What do brakes convert kinetic energy into?

3. What does 'ABS' stand for?

Answers:
1. Disc brake 2. Heat energy 3. Anti-lock braking system

Special speeds

90 Speed crops up where many people would not think about it. These special uses and examples of speed range from making music to catching people who are driving over the speed limit, to predicting the weather.

0 Calm Chimney smoke rises straight up

1 Light air Smoke drifts gently

3 Gentle breeze Washing flutters

2 Light breeze Leaves rustle

4 Moderate breeze Paper blows around

91 Fast aircraft may measure their speed in Mach numbers. These compare the speed of an object to the speed of sound under the same conditions of air temperature and pressure. The speed of sound is always Mach 1. An aircraft flying at Mach 0.9 is travelling at nine tenths of the speed of sound. At sea level this is about 1110 kilometres per hour. Very high, in cold thin air, it is 995 kilometres per hour.

▶ A shock wave of air (area of very high pressure) forming around this F-18 Super Hornet shows it is close to going faster than sound.

92 Speed is part of how things vibrate, or move to and fro. This is known as frequency, measured in Hertz (Hz). Twenty Hz is 20 vibrations per second, the lowest or deepest sound human ears detect. A piano's highest or top note is 4186 Hz.

▼ High-pitched or high-frequency sounds have shorter waves than low or deep ones.

High pitch (short wave)

Low pitch (long wave)

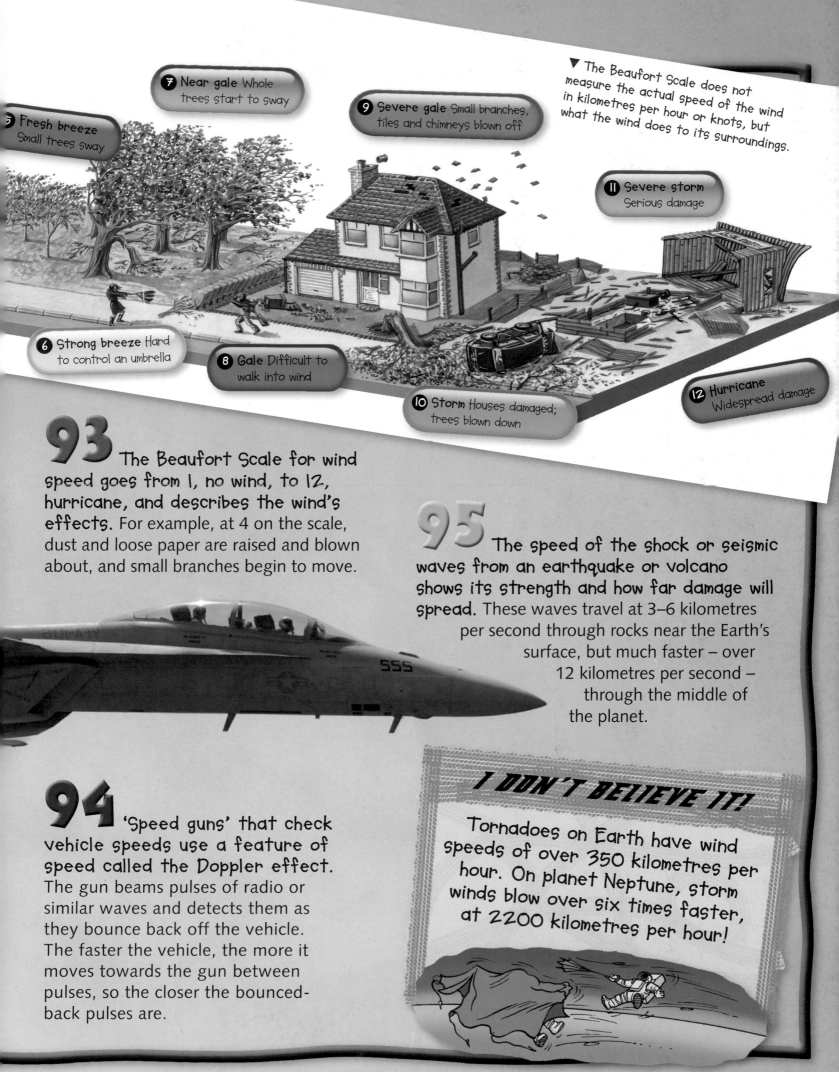

7 **Near gale** Whole trees start to sway

9 **Severe gale** Small branches, tiles and chimneys blown off

▼ The Beaufort Scale does not measure the actual speed of the wind in kilometres per hour or knots, but what the wind does to its surroundings.

5 **Fresh breeze** Small trees sway

11 **Severe storm** Serious damage

6 **Strong breeze** Hard to control an umbrella

8 **Gale** Difficult to walk into wind

10 **Storm** Houses damaged; trees blown down

12 **Hurricane** Widespread damage

93 The Beaufort Scale for wind speed goes from 1, no wind, to 12, hurricane, and describes the wind's effects. For example, at 4 on the scale, dust and loose paper are raised and blown about, and small branches begin to move.

95 The speed of the shock or seismic waves from an earthquake or volcano shows its strength and how far damage will spread. These waves travel at 3–6 kilometres per second through rocks near the Earth's surface, but much faster – over 12 kilometres per second – through the middle of the planet.

94 'Speed guns' that check vehicle speeds use a feature of speed called the Doppler effect. The gun beams pulses of radio or similar waves and detects them as they bounce back off the vehicle. The faster the vehicle, the more it moves towards the gun between pulses, so the closer the bounced-back pulses are.

I DON'T BELIEVE IT!

Tornadoes on Earth have wind speeds of over 350 kilometres per hour. On planet Neptune, storm winds blow over six times faster, at 2200 kilometres per hour!

Ultimate speed

96 Modern science tells us that the fastest possible speed is the speed of light. It is about 300,000 kilometres per second (actually 299,792,458 metres per second). This means light could go around the Earth seven times in less than a second. As far as we know, nothing can travel faster.

97 The speed of light is usually written as the symbol *c*. It is so important that it is the only speed that is fixed or constant, everywhere at any time. In fact, it is more constant than time itself. Scientists explain weird events in deep space by saying that time can go faster or slower, but the speed of light cannot.

▼ The fastest-ever human-made objects, capable of reaching 252,792 kilometres per hour, were two *Helios* spacecraft sent to study the Sun in 1974.

QUIZ

1. Which are faster — radio waves, microwaves or X-rays?

2. Does light go slowest in space, air or water?

3. How many days in a light-year?

Answers:
1. They all travel at the speed of light 2. In water 3. A light-year measures distance, not time. A light year is 9.4 million million kilometres

98 Light speed is not only for light waves. It is for all similar kinds of waves, known as electromagnetic waves. These include radio waves, microwaves, infra-red and ultra-violet rays, X-rays and gamma rays. Also the speed of light is usually measured in a vacuum (a space empty of matter). It is slightly slower in air, and even slower in water.

▲ Like all forms of light, laser light beams — such as those seen here at a concert — go as fast as radio, X-rays and all other waves made of electrical and magnetic energy.

99 Will it ever be possible to exceed light speed? Some experts suggest ideas such as 'warp drive'. Instead of light passing through space, space is bent or warped to pass around the light beam.

100 Going faster than the speed of light would lead to many strange events. One idea is that as you approach light speed, time slows down. At light speed, time stops. So faster than light could allow you to travel back in time. Then you could read this book all over again and be just as amazed!

▲ In science fiction on TV and in movies, craft such as Star Trek's *Enterprise* sometimes go faster than light — perhaps when being pulled into a massive black hole.

Index